Oxford English for Cambridge Primary

Workbook

2

Sarah Snashall

OXFORD
UNIVERSITY PRESS

OXFORD
UNIVERSITY PRESS

Great Clarendon Street, Oxford, OX2 6DP, United Kingdom

Oxford University Press is a department of the University of Oxford. It furthers the University's objective of excellence in research, scholarship, and education by publishing worldwide. Oxford is a registered trade mark of Oxford University Press in the UK and in certain other countries

© Oxford University Press 2016

The moral rights of the authors have been asserted

First published in 2016

All rights reserved. No part of this publication may be reproduced, stored in a retrieval system, or transmitted, in any form or by any means, without the prior permission in writing of Oxford University Press, or as expressly permitted by law, by licence or under terms agreed with the appropriate reprographics rights organization. Enquiries concerning reproduction outside the scope of the above should be sent to the Rights Department, Oxford University Press, at the address above.

You must not circulate this work in any other form and you must impose this same condition on any acquirer

British Library Cataloguing in Publication Data
Data available

978-0-19-836630-0

10 9 8 7 6

Paper used in the production of this book is a natural, recyclable product made from wood grown in sustainable forests. The manufacturing process conforms to the environmental regulations of the country of origin.

Printed in Great Britain by Ashford Colour Press Ltd., Gosport

Acknowledgements
The questions, example answers, marks awarded and/or comments that appear in this book were written by the authors. In examination, the way marks would be awarded to answers like this might be different.

The publishers would like to thank the following for permissions to use their photographs:

Cover: GK Hart/Vikki Hart / Getty Images; p70a: Jason Isley -Scubazoo/Science Faction/Corbis; p70b: Mike Parry/Minden Pictures/FLPA; p73: Jason Isley -Scubazoo/Science Faction/Corbis; p78: Jason Isley -Scubazoo/Science Faction/Corbis;

Artwork is by: Andy Catling, Meg Hunt, Cathy Ionescu, Tamara Joubert, Alan Marks, Gustavo Mazali, Zack Mcloughlin, Jess Mikhail, Dusan Pavlic, Luciano Navarro Powell, Q2A Media Services Pvt. Ltd, Yannick Robert, Kimberley Scott

The author and publisher are grateful for permission to reprint the following copyright material:

Valerie Bloom: 'Water Everywhere' from *Let Me Touch the Sky: Selected Poems for Children* (Macmillans Children's Books, 2000), copyright © Valerie Bloom 2000, reprinted by permission of the author c/o Eddison Pearson Ltd.

Paul Cookson: 'My Football' from *Pants on Fire* (Macmillan Children's Books, 2005), copyright © Paul Cookson 2005, reprinted by permission of the author.

Becca Heddle: *Yoshi The Stonecutter* (ORT Traditional Tales, OUP, 2011), text copyright © Rebecca Heddle 2011, reprinted by permission of the author and publisher.

Eithne Massey: *The Dreaming Tree* (O'Brien, 2009), copyright © Eithne Massey 2009, reprinted by permission of The O'Brien Press Ltd, Dublin.

Roger McGough: 'Allivator' from *An Imaginary Menagerie* (Frances Lincoln, 2011), copyright © Roger McGough 2011, reprinted by permission of Frances Lincoln Ltd.

Michael Morpurgo: extracts from *The Dancing Bear* (HarperCollins, 1994), copyright © Michael Morpurgo 1994, reprinted by permission of HarperCollins Publishers Ltd.

Chloe Rhodes: extract from *Project X: Rubbish!* (OUP, 2009), copyright © Oxford University Press 2009, reprinted by permission of Oxford University Press.

Any third party use of this material, outside of this publication, is prohibited. Interested parties should apply to the copyright holders indicated in each case.

Although we have made every effort to trace and contact all copyright holders before publication this has not been possible in all cases. If notified, the publisher will rectify any errors or omissions at the earliest opportunity.

Links to third party websites are provided by Oxford in good faith and for information only. Oxford disclaims any responsibility for the materials contained in any third party website referenced in this work.

Contents

1. **Fiction** New friends — 4
2. **Non-fiction** Party time! — 14
3. **Poetry** Everyday poems — 24
4. **Fiction** World stories — 32
5. **Non-fiction** How things work — 42
6. **Poetry** Caribbean trip — 52
7. **Fiction** Mountain bear adventure — 60
8. **Non-fiction** Animal world — 70
9. **Poetry** Wordplay poems — 80

Learning reflections — 88

Word Cloud dictionary — 89

New Word List — 96

Fiction **Reading and comprehension • Student Book pages 10–15**

1 New friends

Read this extra part of the story *The Dreaming Tree* by Eithne Massey.

Amanda was jumping up and down. She wanted to talk to Vovó.

"Let your sister have a go on the phone," said his mother. "This is costing Vovó a fortune."

Amanda got on the telephone to her grandmother. She told her all about her new friend. Her friend was called Aoife (Eefa). Tomorrow, Amanda was going to Aoife's birthday party. When she got off the phone she wanted to show Roberto and their mother the new dance she had learned at school.

"You are showing off," said Roberto.

Amanda didn't care what he said. She kept smiling and dancing.

"She is not showing off," said his mother. "Amanda is a good dancer. You are good at football. Why don't you show the boys at school how good you are? It's ok to be proud of what you can do. I am proud that I am such a good gardener!"

Fiction Reading • Student Book pages 10–15 and 16

Roberto's mother was a very good gardener. Even though there was no garden in the apartment, there was a balcony. Roberto's mother had filled it with lots of bright flowers. It was the brightest balcony in the block. Roberto's mother loved bright colours. She made Roberto wear blue and red and yellow shirts.

Roberto hated to look different from everyone else.

A Circle the correct answer to each question.

1 When is Amanda going to the birthday party?

   today   tomorrow   next week

2 What does Roberto's mother say Roberto is good at?

   dancing   talking   football

3 Who is a good gardener?

   Roberto's mother   Amanda   Roberto's grandmother

5

Fiction Comprehension • Student Book pages 16–17

B What did Amanda want to do after she got off the phone? Choose the correct answer and complete the sentence.

> show them the flowers she had planted

> play football with Roberto

> show Roberto and her mother the new dance

Amanda wanted to _____

_____

C Why do you think Roberto tells Amanda she is showing off?

_____

_____

_____

_____

_____

Fiction Spelling and phonics • Student Book page 19

Word detective

A Find these words with the 'ar' letter group from the story on pages 4–5 in the word search. One has been done for you.

f	p	w	b	h	w	p	w	c
c	a	r	e	d	g	b	l	n
p	r	g	j	a	w	d	e	s
n	t	f	p	n	q	r	a	f
v	y	i	a	r	e	p	r	r
m	j	y	k	m	w	s	n	p
z	g	a	r	d	e	n	e	r
w	i	v	h	k	l	z	d	m
q	n	p	w	e	a	r	f	o

party
learned
care
are
gardener
wear

B Read the words you found in the word search aloud. Write the three words that have the long /ar/ vowel sound on the lines below.

_____ _____ _____

C Think of one word with the long /ar/ vowel sound that has the letter group 'al' and one that is spelled with just an 'a'. Write the words on the lines below.

_____

_____

The /ar/ sound can be spelled with the letter groups 'ar' and 'al', or with just an 'a'.

Fiction Vocabulary and grammar • Student Book page 18

Connectives

A Choose one of these connectives to complete each sentence.

and   but

1 Amanda spoke to her grandmother _____ she told her about her new friend.

2 He said Amanda was showing off _____ his mother disagreed.

B Use a connective to connect these two sentences.

Roberto is good at football. He has no one to play with.

_____

_____

C Complete this sentence with an idea of your own.

Robert's mother asked him to stop talking because _____

_____

Fiction Vocabulary • Student Book page 20

Descriptions

Read this extra part of Roberto's story.

Roberto and Amanda were on their way home from school. It was only a short walk through the park. The park was nice. There were lots of trees and flowers. There were lots of children playing. There was a little river.

Roberto had to look after Amanda. She was two years younger than he was. Amanda smiled most of the time. She was not smiling now.

A Find two words or phrases in the story above that describe the park.

_____

_____

B These sentences describe Amanda. Tick the ones that are true.

1 Amanda had lost her schoolbag. ☐

2 She smiled most of the time. ☐

3 She was two years younger than Roberto. ☐

C Think of two other adjectives to describe the park or a park you have visited and write them in a sentence of your own.

_____

_____

Fiction Writing • Student Book page 22

Get writing

Plan a story about moving house and meeting new friends.

Part 1 Main character

What is your character like? (Are they friendly, lonely, happy, mean, unhappy, shy, or something else?)

_____

What does your character like to do? (Do they like to play on the computer/ read/ play outside/talk to friends?)

_____

Did your character have lots of friends where they lived before?

_____

Draw a picture of your character here and write their name at the top.

Part 2 Setting

Where has your character moved to? Choose a setting for your story. Use one of these ideas or think of one of your own.

Write words and phrases to describe your setting here. Is it a city, the countryside or a town? Where do the children play? What is the weather like? Remember to use your exercise book if you need more space.

_____

_____

_____

_____

_____

_____

_____

Fiction Writing • **Student Book page 23**

Part 3 Story plan

Use the questions to help you plan each part of the story.

Make notes on the lines below and use your exercise book.

Beginning
- Why has your character moved house? • Did they move a long way?
- How does your character feel about their new home?

_____

_____

Middle
- What happens? • Are they arriving at a new school for the first time?
- What are the other children like? (Helpful, mean or friendly?)

_____

_____

End
- How does your story finish? • Does your character make friends?
- Are they happy in their new home?

_____

_____

Fiction Assessment

Self-assessment on my learning
Unit 1 New friends

Name _____   Date _____

☺ I understand and can do this well.

😐 I understand but am not confident.

☹ I don't understand and find this difficult.

Learning objective	☺	😐	☹
Reading skills			
I can answer questions about a story.			
I can suggest what a character is feeling.			
I can comment on vocabulary choices.			
Writing skills			
I can use connectives to link ideas and join sentences.			
I can plan a story with a setting, character and events.			
Language (spelling) skills			
I can identify words with the /ar/ sound.			

I would like more help with

_____

_____

13

Non-fiction Reading • Student Book pages 25–26

❷ Party time!

Read these instructions about preparing a party trick.

The Great Coin Trick

You will need:

A clear glass
Two pieces of *blue shiny* paper
Pencil, scissors and glue

A coin
A piece of silver paper
Sticky tape

What to do:

1 Place your glass upside down on one piece of blue paper and draw around it with a pencil.

2 Cut out the circle you have drawn.

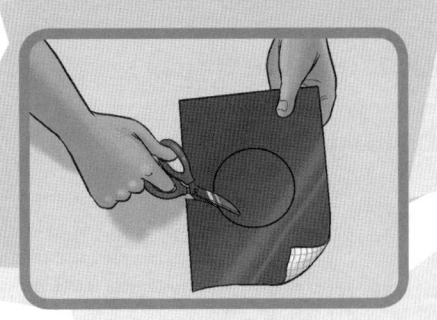

3 Glue the circle onto the opening of the glass.

4 Place the glass and the coin side-by-side on the other piece of blue paper.

5 Roll up the silver paper and tape the sides together to make a tube. The size of the tube needs to be bigger than the glass.

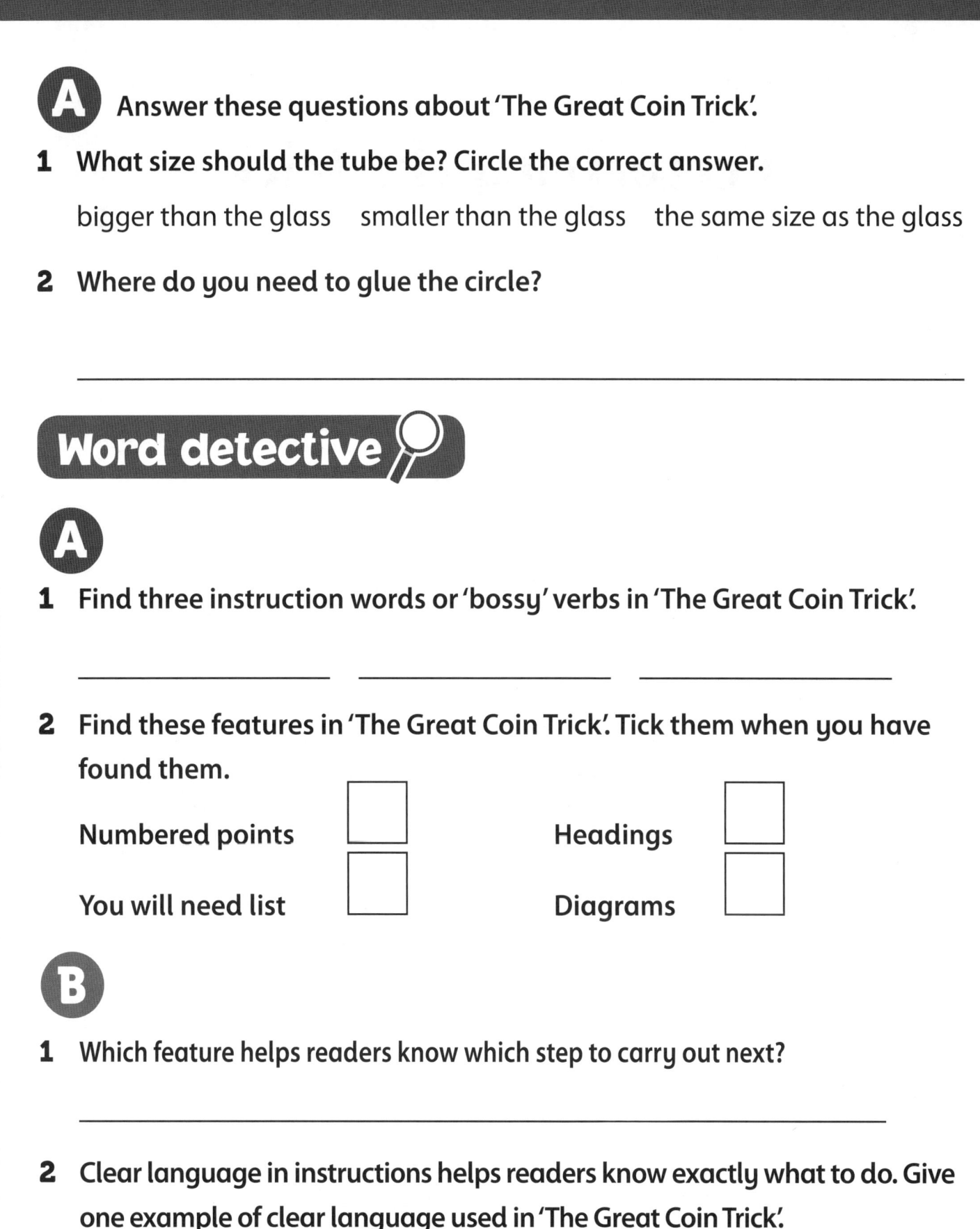

Non-fiction Comprehension and vocabulary • Student Book pages 27, 30 and 31

A Answer these questions about 'The Great Coin Trick'.

1 What size should the tube be? Circle the correct answer.

bigger than the glass   smaller than the glass   the same size as the glass

2 Where do you need to glue the circle?

_____

Word detective

A

1 Find three instruction words or 'bossy' verbs in 'The Great Coin Trick'.

_____   _____   _____

2 Find these features in 'The Great Coin Trick'. Tick them when you have found them.

Numbered points ☐   Headings ☐

You will need list ☐   Diagrams ☐

B

1 Which feature helps readers know which step to carry out next?

_____

2 Clear language in instructions helps readers know exactly what to do. Give one example of clear language used in 'The Great Coin Trick'.

_____

Non-fiction Reading • Student Book pages 28–29

Now read about how to perform the trick.

Performing the trick

1. Invite your friends into the room.
2. Show your friends the glass and the coin.
3. Place the tube over the glass, then wave your hands dramatically.
4. Pick up the glass with the tube and place them over the coin.
5. Remove the tube. The coin will have disappeared.

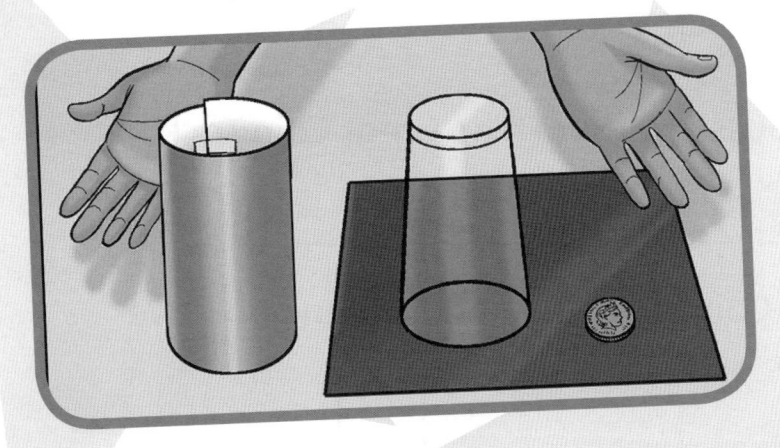

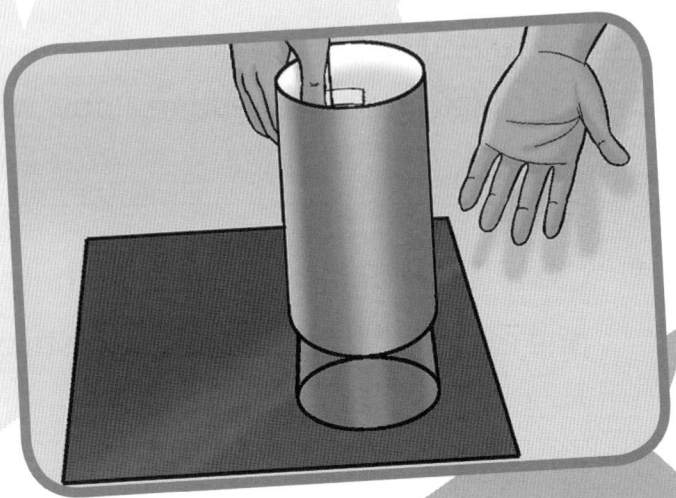

Non-fiction Comprehension • Student Book page 30

A Read 'Performing the trick' and answer these questions.

1 How should you wave your hands?

_____

2 Find a time word in the instructions. Then circle it below.

next   first   then   finally

Remember that time words tell you in which order to do something.

B Now, with someone you know, act out instruction 3, to show you understand the meaning of the word 'dramatically'.

C With someone you know, discuss how you think the trick works. How does the coin disappear? Write your ideas here.

_____

_____

17

Catch the Dragon's Tail game

This traditional Chinese game is great fun for the playground.

You will need:

- Two different-coloured scarves
- At least 10 children

What to do:

1. Divide yourselves into two teams.
2. In your teams, stand in a line and hold on to the shoulders of the child in front of you. The first child in each line is the dragon's head and the last child is the dragon's tail.
3. Give the two dragon tails a scarf each and ask them to tuck it into their waist bands.
4. Each of the two dragon heads must now chase the other dragon's tail.
5. The children in the middle of each dragon must try to stop the other dragon from reaching the tail. They must not break the line.
6. The first dragon to pull out the other dragon's tail is the winner.
7. The dragon heads then go to the back of the line and the game starts again with new heads and tails.

Non-fiction Comprehension • Student Book page 34

A How does a team win the Catch the Dragon's Tail game? Tick the correct answer.

1 By running around in a circle ten times ☐

2 By being the first to pull out the 'dragon's tail' from the other team ☐

3 By making the loudest dragon noises ☐

B What object is used for a dragon's tail in the game?

_____

C Number the following instructions in the right order. Instruction 1 has been done for you.

- **1** Divide yourselves into two teams.
- ◯ Hold on to the shoulders in front of you.
- ◯ The first dragon to pull out the other dragon's tail is the winner.
- ◯ Each dragon head chases the other dragon's tail.
- ◯ The two dragon tails tuck their scarves into their waist bands.

Non-fiction Vocabulary • Student Book page 31

Word detective

A Find four instruction words or phrases from 'Catch the Dragon's Tail game' on page 18 and write them here.

_____

_____

B

1 Add the ending '–ly' to each of these adjectives.

soft____   loud____   slow____

2 Use the new words you made above to complete these sentences.

"Go away!" shouted my brother _____.

The car moved _____ along the busy street.

The girl walked _____ past the sleeping baby.

C Now write your own sentence using a word ending in '–ly'.

_____

_____

Non-fiction Writing • Student Book pages 36–37

Get writing

Part 1 Write an instruction word or phrase from the box to match each of these actions.

> cut out   hit   sing   draw
> jump   paint   stir   kick

21

Non-fiction Writing • Student Book pages 38–39

Part 2 Complete these instructions for making pancakes using the time words below. Add a heading at the top and numbers for each stage.

> Next   Finally   First   Then

What you will need:
100g flour
2 eggs
300ml milk
Mixing bowl, wooden spoon or whisk

☐ _____ put the flour into the bowl.

☐ _____ crack the eggs and tip them into the flour.

☐ _____ pour in the milk and mix everything together.

☐ _____ you are ready to cook pancakes!

C Add the letters –*ly* to one of the words below. Then rewrite one of the steps above using the word you have made.

> careful   slow

22

Non-fiction Assessment

Self-assessment on my learning
Unit 2 Party time!

Name _____ Date _____

☺ I understand and can do this well.

😐 I understand but am not confident.

☹ I don't understand and find this difficult.

Learning objective	☺	😐	☹
Reading skills			
I can find answers to questions by reading a text.			
I can find features of instructions.			
Writing skills			
I can write instruction words.			
I can recognise and use time words.			
Language (spelling) skills			
I can write words ending in –*ly*.			

I would like more help with

_____

_____

3 Everyday poems

Read this poem aloud.

My Football Counting Rhyme

I kicked my football
Once against the wall
Twice in the bathroom
Three times in the hall

Four times in the kitchen
Five times at the door
Six at my sister
Then seven more

Eight against the gate
Nine against the slide
Ten against the greenhouse
And then I had to hide!

Paul Cookson

Poetry Comprehension • Student Book page 42

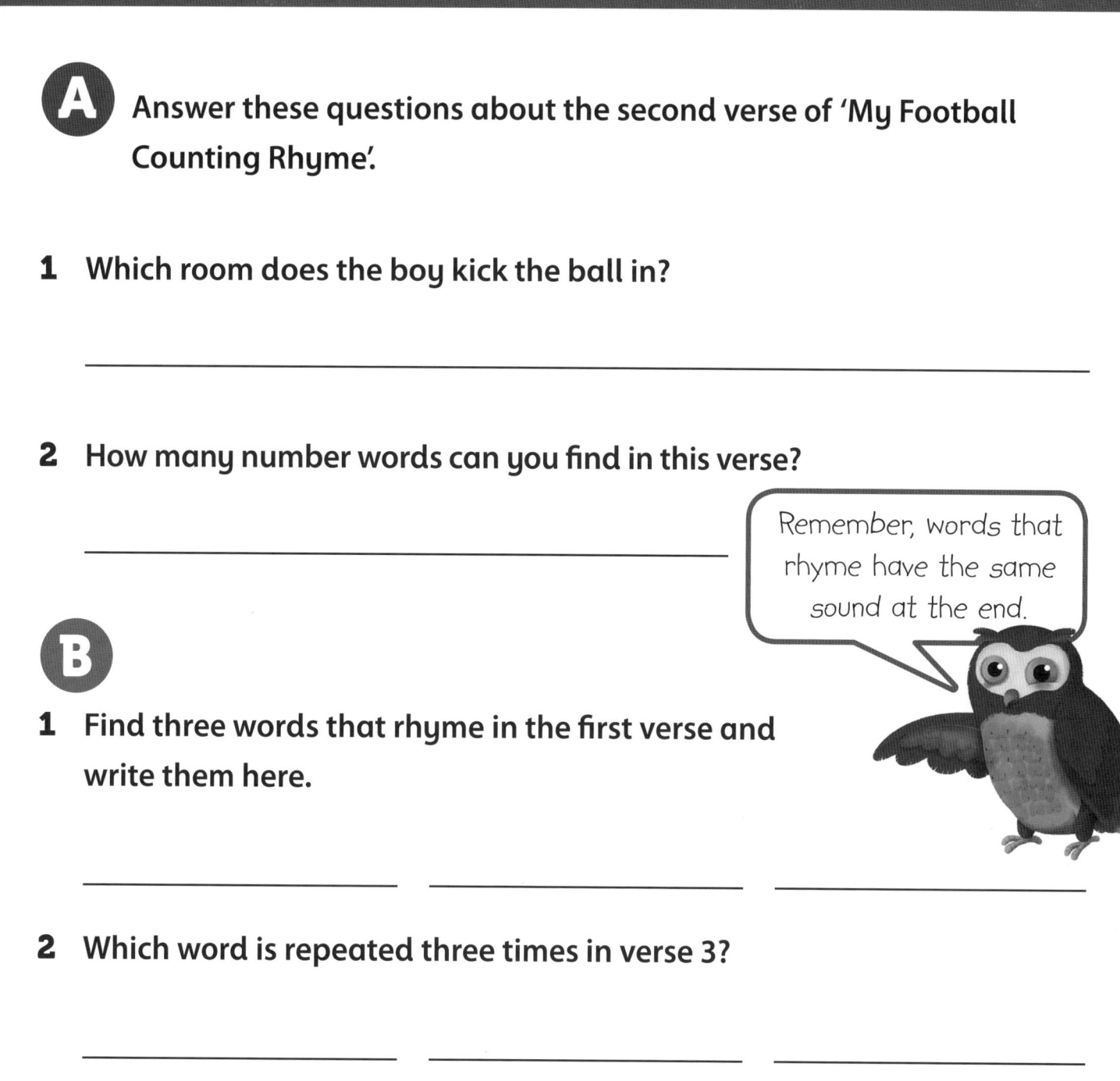

A Answer these questions about the second verse of 'My Football Counting Rhyme'.

1 Which room does the boy kick the ball in?

_____

2 How many number words can you find in this verse?

_____

Remember, words that rhyme have the same sound at the end.

B

1 Find three words that rhyme in the first verse and write them here.

_____   _____   _____

2 Which word is repeated three times in verse 3?

_____   _____   _____

C In 'My Football Counting Rhyme' the boy says he had to hide. Why do you think he felt he had to do this? Do you think he was right to hide, or should he have owned up to breaking the glass?

_____

_____

25

Supermarket

I'm
lost
among a
maze of cans
behind a pyramid
of jams, quite near
asparagus and rice,
close to the Oriental spice,
and just before sardines.
I hear my mother calling, "Joe.
Where are you, Joe? Where did you go?"
And I reply in a voice concealed among
the candied orange peel, and packs of Chocolate Dreams.

Word Cloud
asparagus   concealed
candied   sardines

"I
hear
you, Mother
dear, I'm here –
quite near the ginger ale
and beer, and lost among a
                        maze
                          of cans
                      behind a
                  pyramid of jams
              quite near asparagus
           and rice, close to the
       Oriental spice, and just before sardines."
                          But
                          still
                       my mother
                  calls me, "Joe!
              Where are you, Joe?
            Where did you go?"

"Somewhere
  around asparagus
  that's in a sort of
        broken glass,
          beside a kind of messy jell
            that's near a tower of cans that fell
                and squashed the Chocolate Dreams."

Felice Holman

Poetry Comprehension • Student Book page 50

A Answer these questions about the poem 'Supermarket'.

1 Find words in the poem that rhyme with the words below.

> spice   fell   Joe

_____   _____   _____

2 Which vegetable does Joe say he is quite near?

_____

B

1 How many times does Joe hear his mother calling?

_____

2 Find the phrase 'pyramid of jams' in the poem. What do you think this means?

_____

C How do you think Joe's mother is feeling in the poem? Write your ideas here.

_____

_____

Poetry Vocabulary • Student Book page 43

Word detective

A Draw lines to connect these words and make compound words.

Remember, a compound word is made up of two smaller words which together make a new word.

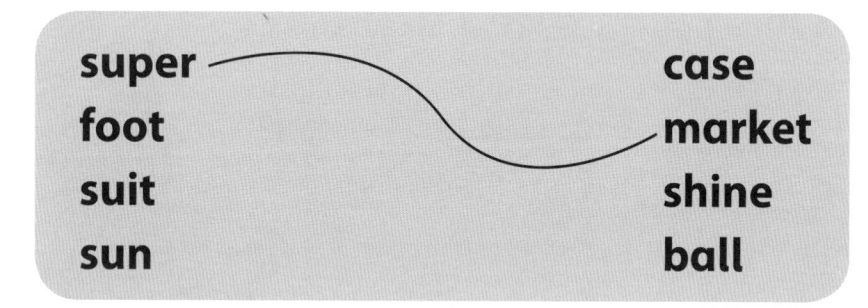

super	case
foot	market
suit	shine
sun	ball

(super—market connected)

B Find one word in the poem 'Supermarket', that has each of the following long vowel sounds.

/igh/   /ee/   /oa/   /ai/   /oi/   /oo/

_____   _____   _____

_____   _____   _____

C Rewrite the following sentence, adding speech marks (" ") around the words that are spoken.

Joe's mother called, Joe, where are you, Joe?

_____

29

Poetry Writing • Student Book page 51

Get writing

Part 1 Complete this poem using any words from the box.

> boring   fun   am snoring
> run   there   everywhere   shout   all about

I think shopping is _____.

When I get to the shops I _____.

Boxes and tins piled high

A squeaky trolley passes by

People here, people _____

Children running _____

At the busy, noisy shops.

Part 2 Think of your own words to rhyme with the words below.

> wait   make   night   day

_____   _____   _____   _____

Poetry Assessment

Self-assessment on my learning
Unit 3 Everyday poems

Name _____   Date _____

☺ I understand and can do this well.

😐 I understand but am not confident.

☹ I don't understand and find this difficult.

Learning objective	☺	😐	☹
Reading skills			
I can hear rhyme in poems.			
Writing skills			
I can choose words to create a new poem.			
Language (spelling) skills			
I can identify long vowel sounds.			
I can join words to make compound words.			

I would like more help with

_____

_____

4 World stories

Read this story.

Yoshi the Stonecutter

A tale from Japan retold by Becca Heddle

Long ago in the mountains of Japan, there lived a stonecutter called Yoshi. He was a poor man with a bent back and hard hands from cutting stone.

People said a spirit lived in the mountains where Yoshi worked. They said it granted wishes. But Yoshi had never seen the spirit.

One day, Yoshi took some stone to a rich man's house. Yoshi loved the rich man's beautiful home, his silk clothes and his clean, soft hands.

"Oh, I wish I could be a rich man," whispered Yoshi.

A cool wind blew and the mountain spirit appeared. It whispered, "Your wish is granted, Yoshi – a rich man you now shall be."

Fiction Reading and comprehension • Student Book 53–55 and 56

When Yoshi got home, his hut had become a fine house. Yoshi was rich. He put away his tools and rested, looking out of the window.

The day grew hot. Yoshi saw a prince ride by. Servants fanned the prince to cool him and shaded him with golden umbrellas.

"I wish I could be a prince," said Yoshi.

The spirit said, "Your wish is granted, Yoshi – a prince you now shall be."

Now Yoshi was a prince, riding in a carriage with servants around him.

A Answer these questions about the story.

1 Where is the story set?

Iraq ☐   Japan ☐   Canada ☐

2 When is the story set?

Last year ☐   Now ☐   Long ago ☐

33

Fiction Comprehension • Student Book pages 56 and 57

B What does Yoshi think will make him happy? Complete these sentences.

1 When Yoshi is a stonecutter he wants to be a rich man because

_____

_____

_____

2 When Yoshi is a rich man he wants to be a prince because

_____

_____

_____

C Do you think Yoshi will be happy when he is a prince? How do you think this story will end? Write your ideas here and then discuss them with your partner.

_____

_____

_____

Word detective

A Find and underline these time words and phrases in the story on pages 32–33. Tick them when you have found them.

Long ago ☐   One day ☐   When ☐   Now ☐

B Find the time words in this word search. The first one has been done for you.

a	w	s	i	n	c	e
s	a	e	w	h	e	n
o	f	t	e	n	f	o
o	t	t	h	e	n	w
n	e	n	i	x	t	e
a	r	l	a	t	e	r
f	i	n	a	l	l	y

1 l _ater_
2 s _____
3 a _____
4 t _____
5 n _____
6 w _____
7 f _____
8 n _____
9 s _____
10 o _____

C Choose three of the time words you found in the word search and use them in three sentences of your own.

_____

_____

_____

35

Fiction Phonics and spelling • Student Book page 58

Long vowel sound /ou/

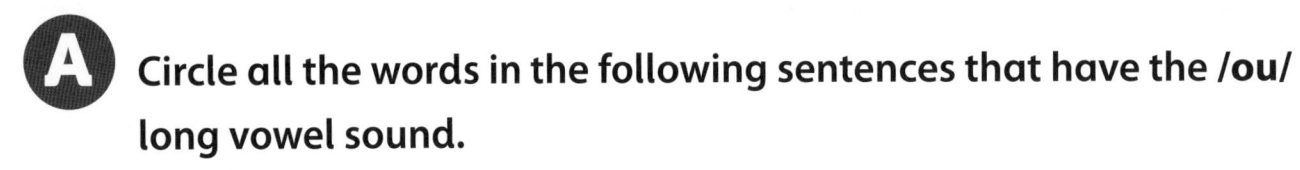

A Circle all the words in the following sentences that have the /ou/ long vowel sound.

1 Long ago in the mountains of Japan, there lived a stonecutter called Yoshi.
2 "Your wish is granted, Yoshi – a rich man you now shall be."
3 When Yoshi got home, his hut had become a fine house.
4 Now Yoshi was a prince, riding in a carriage with servants around him.

B Look at the different spellings for the /ou/ long vowel sound below. Write the words from activity A in the correct circles.

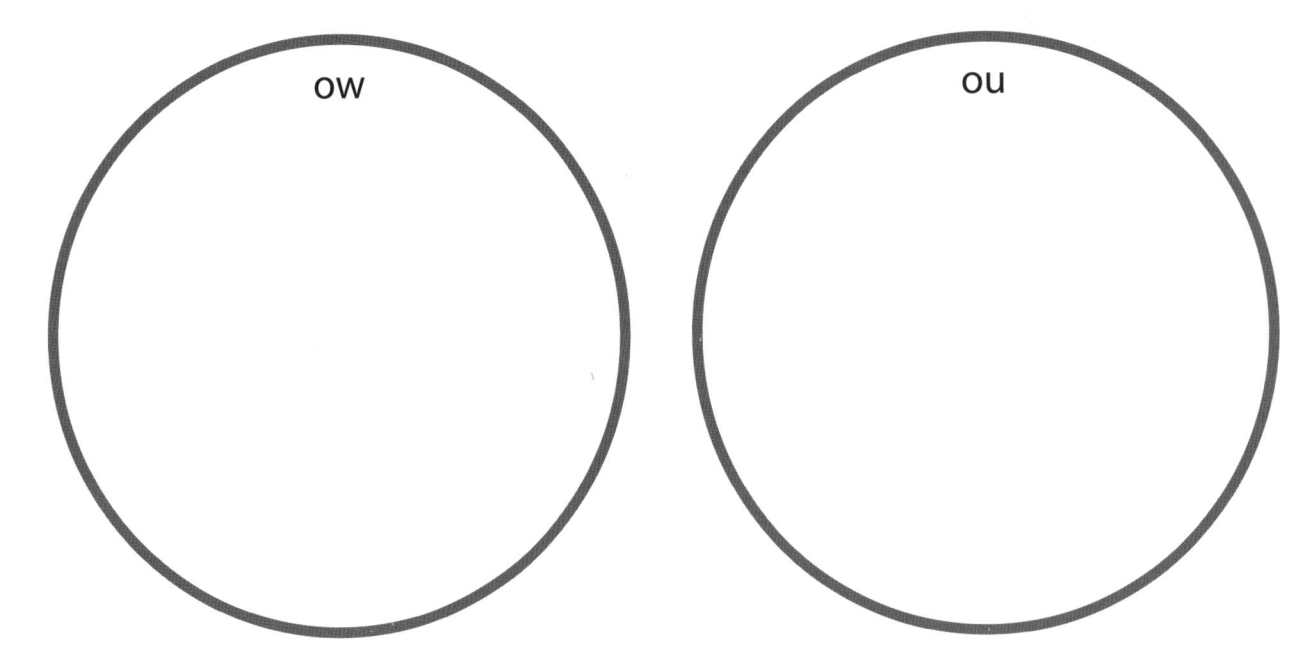

ow

ou

C Choose two of the words with the /ou/ sound that you have written in the circles above and use them in two sentences of your own.

Verbs and tenses

A Complete these sentences using a past tense verb. Then read the sentences aloud to check they make sense.

Remember – a verb is a doing or action word.

1 Oscar _____ over the fence. (jumps/jumped)

2 Rahim _____ away from the house. (walked/walks)

3 Annie _____ in the school play. (dances/danced).

B Use one of the following verbs in the past tense to complete the sentences below.

> play   visit

1 Yesterday, Malik _____ his grandmother.

2 After school, the children _____ in the park.

C Write a sentence about what you did yesterday. You can use any of the verbs in the cloud or choose your own.

> whisper
> shout   look
> pick   watch   talk
> arrive   appear

Yesterday, I _____

_____

Fiction Vocabulary • Student Book page 65

Compound words

A Split these compound words into the two words that make them.

> bedtime   sunflower

1 _____   _____

2 _____   _____

B Use the following words to make three compound words.

> week   light   case   sun   book   end

_____   _____   _____

C Look at the pictures and circle the three words in the word search below. They are all compound words.

s	j	l	f	a	k	x	n	p	w
t	e	n	w	o	e	d	q	k	y
a	p	b	v	u	y	f	h	e	f
t	o	o	t	h	b	r	u	s	h
f	q	c	x	t	o	w	g	i	r
s	u	n	g	l	a	s	s	e	s
d	r	t	s	m	r	z	t	d	x
m	w	r	p	f	d	j	y	e	a

38

Fiction Writing • Student Book pages 67, 68 and 69

Get writing

Plan a story about an animal who has an adventure.

Part 1 Choose an animal from the pictures below or think of one of your own.

Write some interesting words and phrases to describe your animal here. What does your animal look like? What sort of character does he/she have?

_____

_____

Part 2 Choose one of the following settings for your story, or decide on one of your own. Describe the scene using interesting words and phrases.

_____

_____

39

Fiction Writing • Student Book pages 67, 68 and 69

Part 3 Think about what is going to happen in your story. Write notes for each stage.

- What will happen at the beginning of the story? (Will your animal go on a long journey? Will there be a problem to solve?)

  _____

  _____

- What will happen in the middle? (Will your animal get lost? Will he/she meet other characters? Describe them. Will they be in danger?)

  _____

  _____

  _____

- How will the story end?

  _____

  _____

Use your notes to help you write your story in your exercise book. Give your story a title and start with a time phrase. When you write your story, try to form your letters correctly and join up the letters you have practised.

Fiction Assessment

Self-assessment on my learning
Unit 4 World stories

Name _____   Date _____

☺ I understand and can do this well.

😐 I understand but am not confident.

☹ I don't understand and find this difficult.

Learning objective	☺	😐	☹
Reading skills			
I can identify where and when a story is set.			
I can answer questions about a story.			
Writing skills			
I can use time words in sentences and a story.			
I can write a story with a setting and characters.			
I can plan the beginning, middle and end of a story.			
Language (spelling) skills			
I can identify the long vowel sound /ou/ in words.			

I would like more help with

_____

_____

Non-fiction Reading • Student Book pages 71–73

5 How things work

Read this explanation text.

How Glass is Recycled

What happens to your empty drink bottles and food jars when you take them to be recycled? Read on to find out.

1 Glass bottles and jars are put into the recycling bin.

2 When they have reached the recycling plant, all the same coloured bottles and jars are put together.

Non-fiction Reading • Student Book pages 71–73

3 The glass is now cleaned.

Word Cloud
melted   recycled   shaped

4 Then it is melted.

5 The melted glass is shaped into new bottles.

43

Non-fiction Comprehension • Student Book pages 74 and 75

A Read 'How Glass is Recycled' on pages 42 and 43.
Tick the sentence that is true.

This text explains how glass is recycled. ☐

This text explains why glass is recycled. ☐

B Answer these questions.

1 How is glass sorted when it first reaches the recycling plant?

_____

2 What happens to the glass after it has been cleaned?

_____

3 What happens to the glass after it has been melted?

_____

C Think about the order in which glass is recycled. Choose one key word from the text for each part of the diagram below.

_____ → _____ → _____ → _____

Non-fiction Comprehension, phonics and grammar • Student Book pages 75, 77 and 82

Word detective

A Tick each of these features of explanation texts when you find it in 'How Glass is Recycled' on page 42.

Illustration ☐   Numbered steps ☐

Introduction ☐   Present tense ☐

B Look for words in the text that have the long vowel sounds /ee/, /ai/ and /igh/. Find one of each and write them in the correct jars.

/ee/   /ai/   /igh/

C Choose present tense verbs from the box to complete these sentences.

| sort | collect | took | take | sorted | collected |

1 We _____ our empty bottles for recycling.

2 We _____ the glass to a recycling bin.

3 People _____ the bottles into different colours.

45

Non-fiction Vocabulary • Student Book page 76

Connectives

A Circle the four connectives in the cloud and write them below.

sorted   and   put
what   but   melted
so   because   why

_____   _____

_____   _____

B Choose the best connective from activity A to complete these sentences.

1 Water is sprayed onto the bottles _____ they are dirty.

2 The glass is melted _____ it can be made into new glass.

C Choose one of the connectives below and then complete the sentence with an idea of your own.

because   so   but

It is important not to drop litter _____

_____

_____

46

Long vowel sounds

A Look at the diagram showing how a plant grows. Choose words from below to write in the correct boxes.

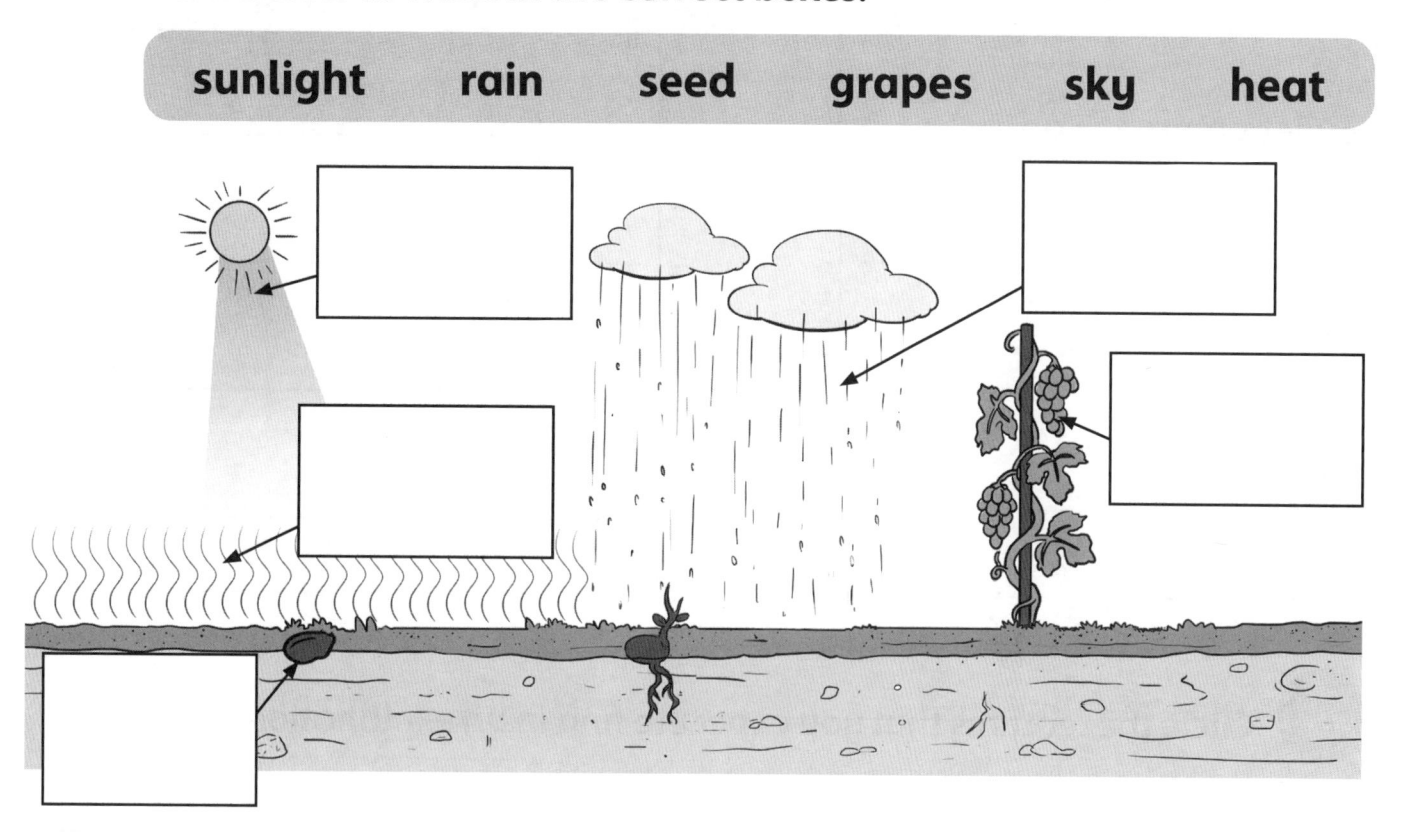

sunlight   rain   seed   grapes   sky   heat

B Say each word from the diagram above aloud. Then write each word in the correct box to show which long vowel sound it has.

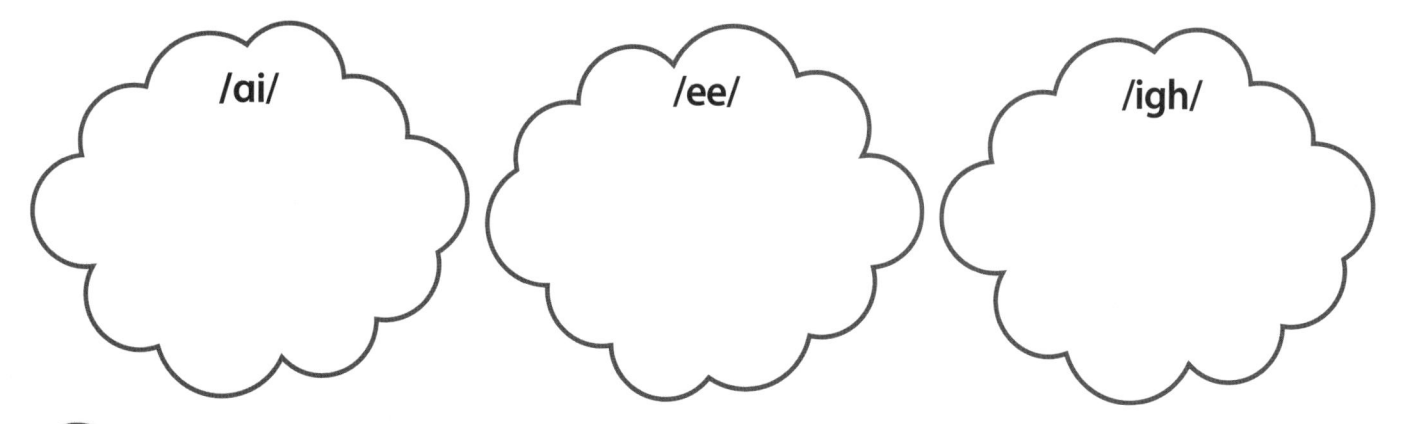

/ai/   /ee/   /igh/

C Think of one more word for each of the long vowel sounds above. Add them to the clouds, being careful to spell them correctly.

Non-fiction Comprehension and vocabulary • Student Book pages 75 and 82

Features of explanation texts

A The parts of an explanation have been mixed up. Write them in the correct order.

Bullet points 4, 5 and 6
Introduction
Ending
Title

_____

_____

_____

_____

B Circle the features that you expect to find in an explanation text.

diagrams   charts   rhyming words
captions   characters   technical words

C Tick the sentence that sounds as if it comes from an explanation text.

1 Fox woke up to hear a strange noise. ☐

2 First, the designer creates a plan of how the page will look. ☐

3 First, put the flour into the bowl. ☐

48

Non-fiction Writing • Student Book pages 81, 84 and 85

Get writing

Part 1

Think about how you get ready for school. What do you do first in the morning? Draw simple pictures in the boxes below to show each stage from waking up to arriving at school. Then write key words and phrases about what you are doing at each stage on the lines below the boxes.

1	2

_____   _____

_____   _____

3	4

_____   _____

_____   _____

Non-fiction Writing • Student Book pages 81, 84 and 85

Part 2

Write an explanation of what you do in the mornings, from waking up to arriving at school. Use your pictures and the key words and phrases you wrote on page 49 to help you. Write each stage below.

1 First, I _____

_____

2 Next, _____

_____

3 Then, _____

_____

4 Finally, _____

_____

Non-fiction Assessment

Self-assessment on my learning
Unit 5 How things work

Name _____   Date _____

☺ I understand and can do this well.

😐 I understand but am not confident.

☹ I don't understand and find this difficult.

Learning objective	☺	😐	☹
Reading skills			
I can find the features of explanation texts.			
Writing skills			
I can use connectives to link ideas.			
I can use features of explanation texts in my writing.			
I can make notes using key words and phrases.			
I can use the present tense in explanations.			
Language (spelling) skills			
I can find and spell some words with long vowel sounds.			

I would like more help with

_____

_____

Poetry Reading • Student Book page 91

6 Caribbean trip

Read this poem.

Water Everywhere

There's water on the ceiling,
    And water on the wall,
There's water in the bedroom,
    And water in the hall,
There's water on the landing,
    And water on the stair,
Whenever Daddy takes a bath
    There's water everywhere.

Valerie Bloom

Word Cloud
landing

A Answer these questions about the poem on page 52.

1 Who takes a bath? _____

2 Where is the poem's title repeated in the poem? Circle the correct answer.

In the first line   In the second line   In the last line

B Look at the picture and write in the boxes to show all the places where the water is. Use the words from the poem to help you.

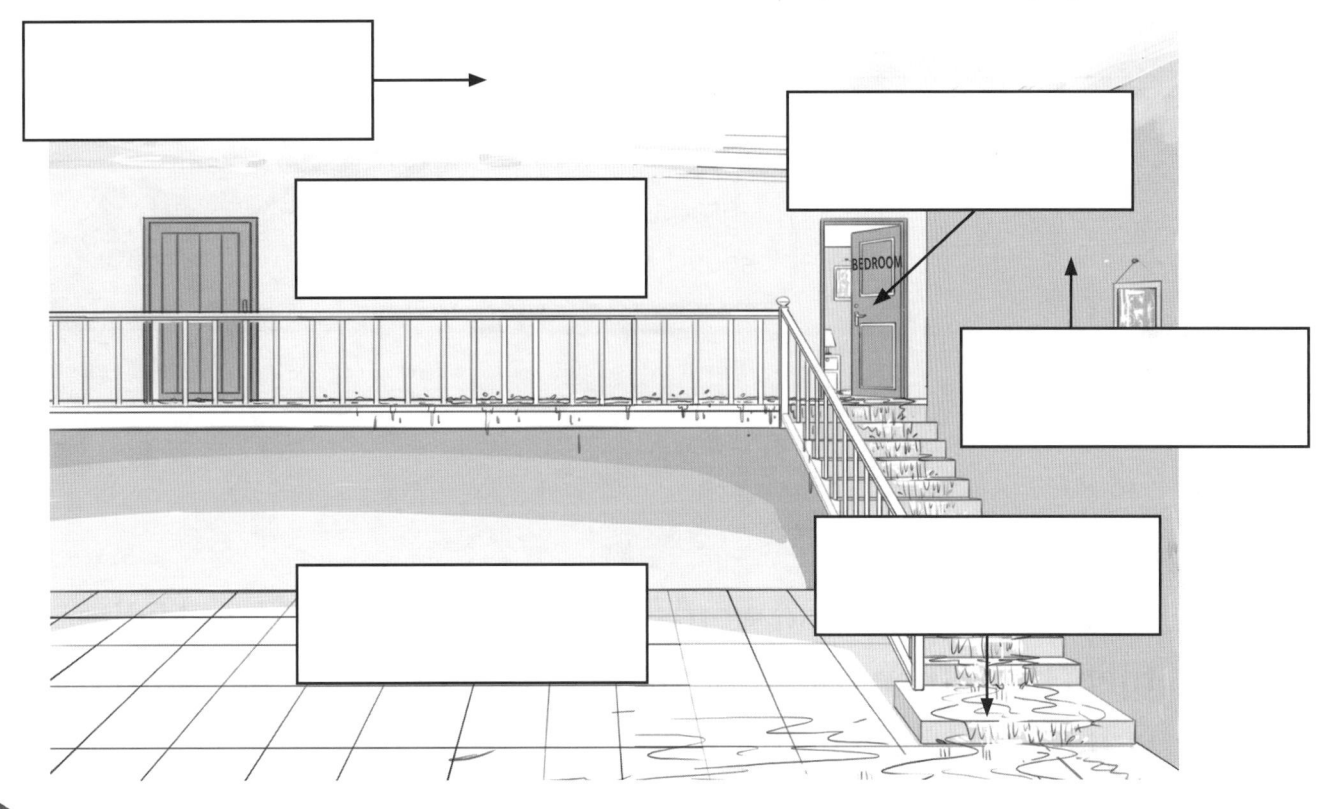

C Do you think the poem has a strong rhyming pattern? Explain your answer.

_____

_____

Poetry Vocabulary • Student Book pages 89 and 93

Word detective

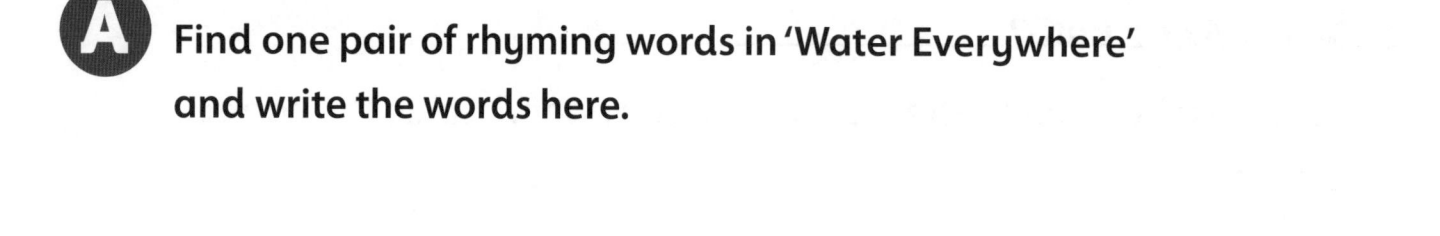

A Find one pair of rhyming words in 'Water Everywhere' and write the words here.

_____   _____

B Find a line in the poem that includes two words that begin with the same sound. Write the line here.

_____

> Say the line aloud a few times, listening to the sound that is repeated.

C Find three compound words in 'Water Everywhere' and write them here. Then count the number of syllables in the words and write the number in the box.

1 _____ ☐

2 _____ ☐

3 _____ ☐

54

Poetry Vocabulary • Student Book pages 89 and 93

Rhyme and rhythm

A Draw lines to match the words that rhyme.

tree	standing
flower	square
landing	spice
skim	breeze
fish	bee
rice	shower
fair	swim
squeeze	dish

B Show how these words can be split up into syllables. The first one has been done for you.

ceil/ing   landing   always   mango   between
finished   coconut   sometimes

C Clap the rhythm of each line below. Then count the number of syllables in each line. Write the number in the box.

The red crabs dance ☐   In water you swim ☐

And then I had to hide! ☐   I won't forget to write ☐

Children playing in the park ☐

Poetry Vocabulary • Student Book page 93

Adjectives

A Find the five adjectives in the box. Circle each one. One has been done for you.

Remember – an adjective describes a person, a place or a thing.

blue   soft   hat   small   boy
house   good   (round)   papaya   teacher

B Read these pairs of sentences. For each pair, tick the sentence that includes an adjective and underline the adjective.

☐ The children stood in a circle.   ☐ The children stood in a large circle.

☐ Sam painted a colourful picture.   ☐ Sam painted a picture.

☐ A green bird landed on the wall.   ☐ A bird landed on the wall.

C Add an adjective of your own to the following sentences to fill the gaps.

1   The teacher read a story to the class under the _____ tree.

2   Water flowed down the _____ staircase.

Sounds and words

A Draw lines to match the words that start with the same sound.

crab   giraffe
walk   wall
slide   creeping
giant   fish
flying   slipper

B Choose two words from the box to make sentence 1 and 2 more interesting. Then add two words of your own to sentence 3.

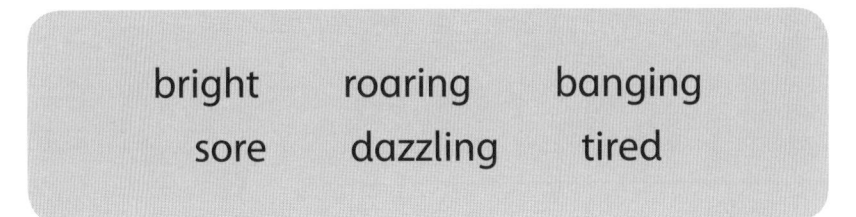

> bright   roaring   banging
> sore   dazzling   tired

1 Suddenly I heard a _____ noise.

2 The _____ light hurt our _____ eyes.

3 The _____ bear stumbled into the _____ river.

C Choose one pair of words you matched in activity A and say them aloud. Try to create a picture in your mind. Then write a sentence using both words. Make it as interesting as you can by adding adjectives or other words that start with the same sound.

_____

_____

Poetry Writing • Student Book page 97

Get writing

Complete this poem about porridge. Use some of the words and phrases from the box, or use words of your own. Think of a title for the poem and add it on line line at the top.

> Porridge is a type of food made from oatmeal, boiled with water or milk to make a thick paste.

flowing	everywhere	all around
on the chair	on the floor	behind the door
watch it ooze	under my shoes	

_____

Porridge growing

Porridge _____

Porridge pouring _____

Porridge on the table

Porridge _____

There's slimy porridge _____

And great big blobs _____

I wish I could just stop it now.

Oh help, I've slipped and fallen down!

I am a porridge man.

58

Poetry Assessment

Self-assessment on my learning
Unit 6 Caribbean trip

Name _____   Date _____

☺ I understand and can do this well.

😐 I understand but am not confident.

☹ I don't understand and find this difficult.

Learning objective	☺	😐	☹
Reading skills			
I can find words that rhyme.			
I can find words that start with the same sound.			
I can clap a line to hear the rhythm.			
I can find adjectives.			
Writing skills			
I can use given words to create a new poem.			
Language (spelling) skills			
I can split compound words into parts.			
I can find the syllables in a word.			

I would like more help with

_____

_____

7 Mountain bear adventure

Read this passage from *The Dancing Bear* by Michael Morpurgo.

Roxanne has adopted a wild bear. A pop star called Niki has realised Roxanne is a wonderful singer and wants her to leave her village and her bear, Bruno, behind. Roxanne's teacher tells the story.

… As night fell, I went off for my usual walk. I was going back towards the square, when I saw Bruno pacing up and down in his cage as he always did when he was upset. I went over to him and sang a little, trying to calm him down. …

And then Roxanne was beside me. She put a hand on my arm.

"I need you to tell me what to do," she said. … "When they go tomorrow Niki wants me to go with him. I'm going to be a singer. Niki says I sing well enough to be famous. Do you think I do?"

"Of course you do," I said. It was an honest answer.

"I think I want to go, but I'm not sure."…

"You must do what you want, Roxanne," I said. … "I can't tell you what to do any more."…

"Then I shall go. I've talked to Bruno. I've told him. He understands." …

We were all there early the next morning and said our goodbyes to the film crew and to Roxanne … Roxanne crouched down by Bruno's cage, a battered brown suitcase beside her. She clung to the bars.

Fiction Reading and comprehension • Student Book pages 100–105 and 106–107

"I'll be back," I heard her whisper. "I promise."

And then she got up and came over to me, wiping the tears from her eyes.

"Look after him for me," she said. Then she was gone.

A Answer these questions about the story.

1 What does the teacher do to try to calm Bruno down?

_____

2 What does Roxanne promise Bruno?

_____

B Read the sentences and tick the two that are true.

Roxanne asks her teacher what she should do. ☐

The teacher tells Roxanne to leave the village. ☐

Roxanne wants the teacher to look after Bruno when she leaves. ☐

C How do you think Roxanne feels about leaving her village? Write your ideas here.

_____

_____

Fiction Vocabulary and spelling • Student Book pages 108, 109 and 110

Word detective

A Find two time words or phrases in the story on pages 60 and 61 and write them below.

_____   _____

B Match the words and phrases on the left with the words that are used to describe them in the story.

suitcase   honest

Bruno's breathing   battered brown

answer   hard

C

1 Turn the following words into adverbs by adding '–ly' and then use the words in two sentences of your own.

   usual   calm

_____

_____

2 Find one word that ends in '-ful' on page 60 and then use the word in a sentence of your own.

_____

Words ending in '–ly' and '–ful'

A Find and circle each of these words in the word search.

> slow care happy
> plenty simple forget

s	w	f	o	r	g	e	t
i	q	n	w	j	f	m	z
m	n	q	p	z	w	v	p
p	s	c	h	t	n	s	l
l	h	a	p	p	y	d	e
e	v	r	d	l	h	n	n
p	d	e	b	t	m	h	t
s	l	o	w	q	v	a	y

> Remember, if a word ends in 'y' (e.g. easy, beauty), change the 'y' to 'i' before adding '–ly' or '–ful' (easily, beautiful). If a word ends in 'le' (e.g. gentle), drop the 'e' before adding '–ly' (gently).

B Add '–ly' or '–ful' to each of the words from the word search and write the new words here.

_____ _____ _____

_____ _____ _____

63

Fiction **Vocabulary** • Student Book page 109

Time words and phrases

A Circle the time words and phrases in the box below.

> why   after that   because   easy
> then   later   how   grasp   every day
> but   next   often

B Choose time words and phrases from activity A to complete these sentences or use words of your own.

1 _____ Fatima gets out of bed and eats breakfast.

Remember to use a capital letter to start a sentence.

2 _____ she packs her school bag.

3 _____ she puts her shoes on and leaves the house.

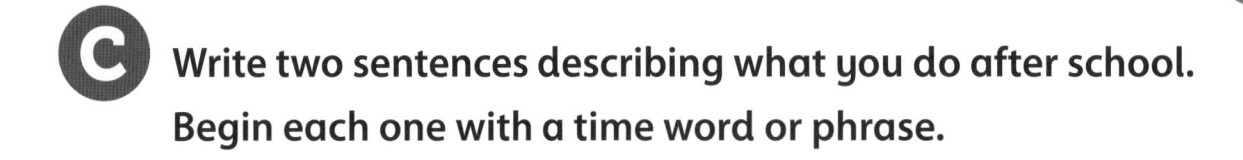

C Write two sentences describing what you do after school. Begin each one with a time word or phrase.

_____

_____

Fiction Vocabulary • Student Book page 110

Descriptions

A Draw lines to link the words in the circles to the words that describe them.

tasty   fierce   tiny   powerful   fruity   timid

(banana)   (mouse)   (lion)

B Think about the bear in the story 'The Dancing Bear' on pages 60–61. Circle the words and phrases which describe him.

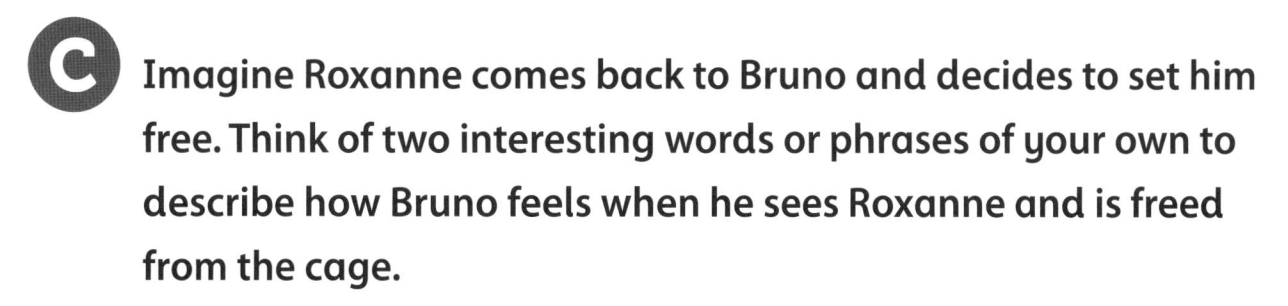

happy

upset

shut in a cage

small and frightened

calm

likes to sing

likes Roxanne

free

C Imagine Roxanne comes back to Bruno and decides to set him free. Think of two interesting words or phrases of your own to describe how Bruno feels when he sees Roxanne and is freed from the cage.

_____

_____

65

Fiction Writing • Student Book pages 111, 112 and 113

Get writing

Imagine a girl or boy is visiting a zoo or animal park and an animal speaks to them. This is the start of their animal adventure!

Part 1 Setting

Think about the setting of the adventure. Is it a zoo in a city or a large animal park in the countryside? Are the animals in cages or can they wander in fields? What kind of animals live there? Draw the setting here and write some interesting words and phrases to describe it.

Part 2 Character

What is your character called? Describe him or on the lines below.
Do they love animals? Draw them in the frame.

_____

_____

_____

_____

_____

Which animal talks to your character? Describe the animal on the lines below and write some words it says. Draw the animal in the box.

_____

_____

_____

_____

Fiction Writing • Student Book pages 111, 112 and 113

Part 3 Story plan

Use these questions to help you plan your story.

Beginning

How does the adventure begin?

_____

_____

Middle

What happens next?

_____

_____

End

How does the story end?

_____

_____

When you have finished, read your story plan aloud to someone else. Can the plan be improved?

Fiction Assessment

Self-assessment on my learning

Unit 7 Mountain bear adventure

Name _____   Date _____

☺ I understand and can do this well.

😐 I understand but am not confident.

☹ I don't understand and find this difficult.

Learning objective	☺	😐	☹
Reading skills			
I can answer questions about the story.			
Writing skills			
I can use time words in sentences.			
I can plan a story with a beginning, middle and end.			
I can include words that are spoken in a story.			
Language (spelling) skills			
I can spell words ending in –*ly* and –*ful*.			

I would like more help with

_____

_____

8 Animal world

Amazing Leatherback Turtle Facts

Prehistoric animals

Turtles have lived on Earth for 150 million years – since the time of the dinosaurs!

Longest journey

Leatherback turtles travel thousands of kilometres from the beaches where they lay their eggs to the oceans where they catch jellyfish.

Turtles in danger

Leatherback turtles are in danger because people collect their eggs to eat. Some turtles also get caught in fishing nets and others die when they eat plastic bags, thinking they are jellyfish.

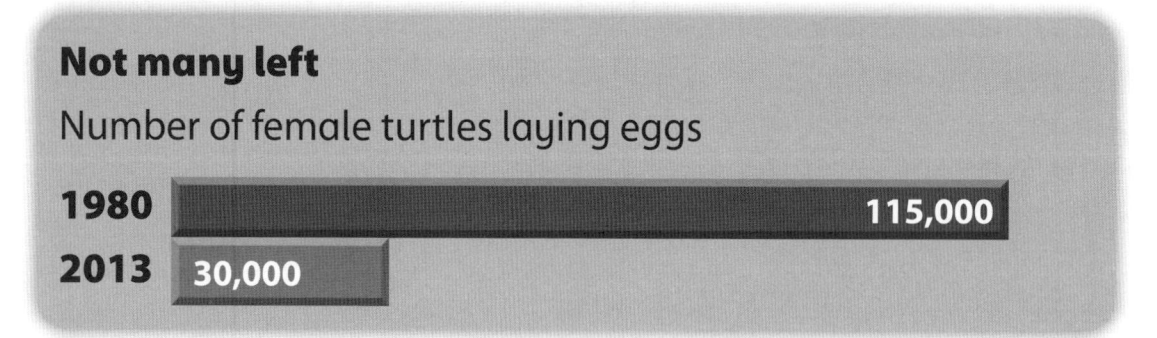

Not many left
Number of female turtles laying eggs

Year	Number
1980	115,000
2013	30,000

Leatherback turtles can dive as deep as 1,000 metres under the sea. That's about the length of 10 football pitches!

Baby turtles have a dangerous journey to the sea.

Non-fiction Comprehension • Student Book pages 118, 121 and 125

One in a thousand

A female leatherback turtle lays about 1,000 eggs. However, not all the eggs will hatch and only about one in a thousand eggs will become a grown-up turtle. Lots of animals like to eat turtles.

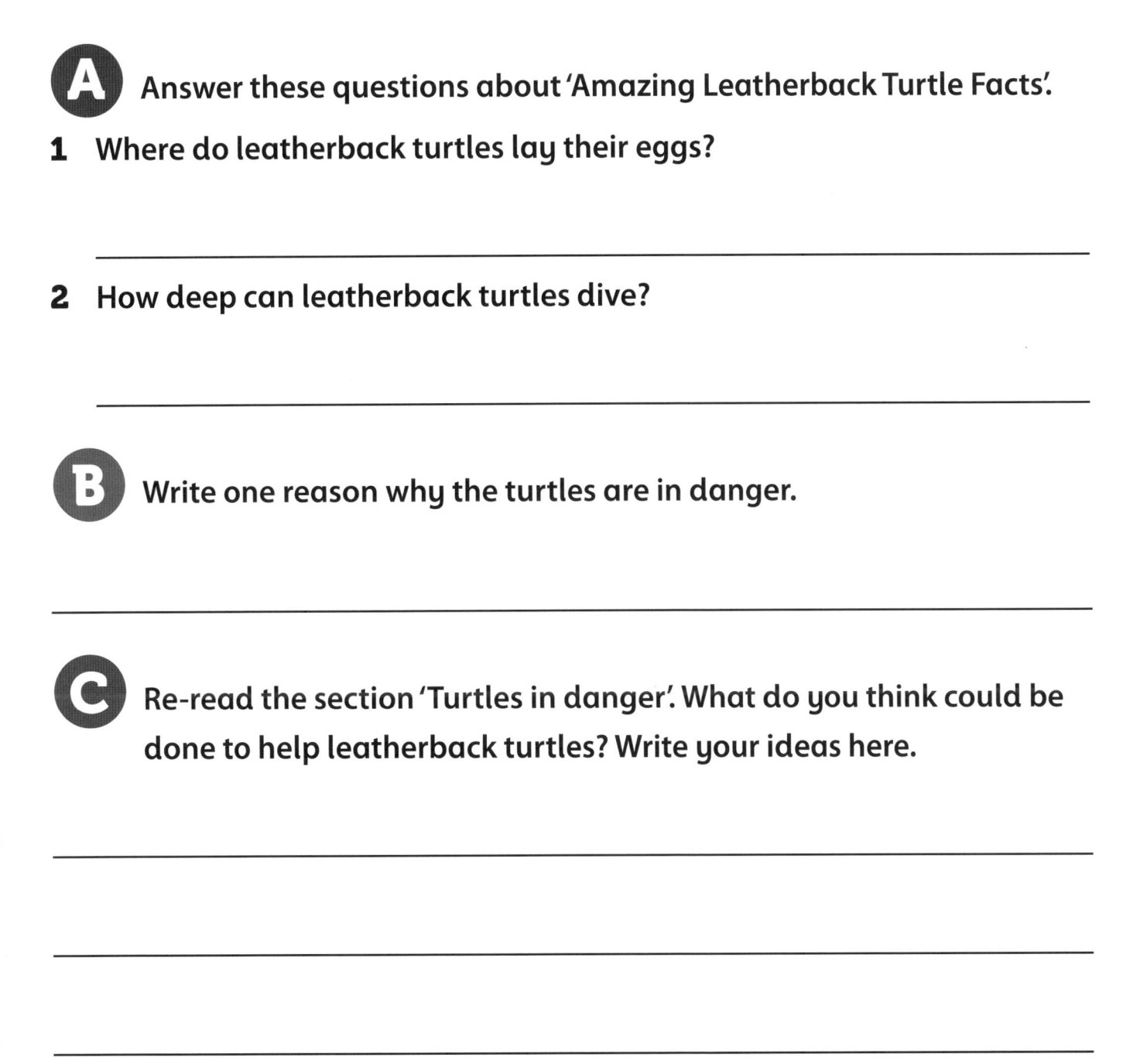

A Answer these questions about 'Amazing Leatherback Turtle Facts'.

1 Where do leatherback turtles lay their eggs?

　

2 How deep can leatherback turtles dive?

　

B Write one reason why the turtles are in danger.

　

C Re-read the section 'Turtles in danger'. What do you think could be done to help leatherback turtles? Write your ideas here.

Non-fiction Grammar and vocabulary • Student Book pages 119 and 126–127

Word detective

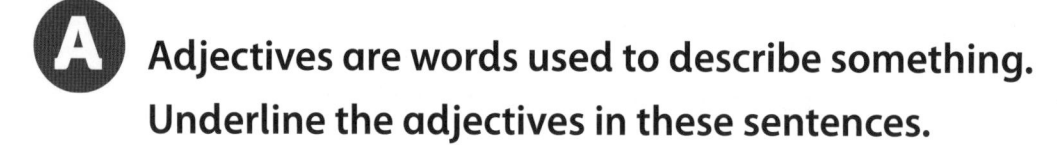

A Adjectives are words used to describe something. Underline the adjectives in these sentences.

1 Female turtles lay eggs.

2 It is a dangerous journey to the sea.

3 They die when they eat plastic bags.

B Write the correct present tense verb in each sentence.

Reports about living things are written in the present tense.

1 Leatherback turtles _____ thousands of kilometres. (travels/travelled/travel)

2 They _____ their eggs on the beaches. (lay/lays/laid)

3 Leatherback turtles _____ jellyfish. (eats/eat/ate)

C Look at the information in the captions on page 70. Write one key word or phrase from each caption on the lines below.

_____

_____

Non-fiction features

A Circle all the non-fiction features you can find in 'Amazing Leatherback Turtle Facts' on pages 70–71.

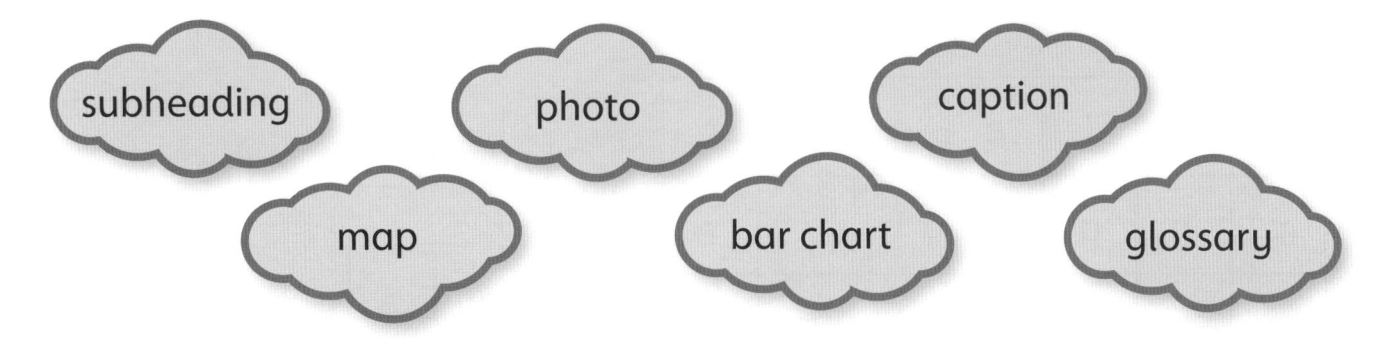

- subheading
- photo
- caption
- map
- bar chart
- glossary

B Match the paragraph description to its subheading. Look back at pages 70–71 to find the paragraphs.

Subheading	Paragraph description
One in a thousand	Explains why turtles die or get injured and tells us that their eggs are removed
Prehistoric animals	Explains how many baby turtles will grow up
Turtles in danger	Tells us how long turtles have lived on Earth

C Write your own subheading for the following paragraph about leatherback turtles.

_____

Conservationists are trying to save leatherback turtles. They are protecting beaches where the turtles nest. They are also helping fishermen to change their ways of fishing so that turtles are not caught in the nets.

Verbs and tenses

A Circle these present tense verbs in the word search. Tick each one when you find it.

r	t	i	e	a	t	c
c	r	a	v	l	i	r
a	a	h	e	l	p	e
t	v	i	s	i	t	a
c	e	d	i	v	e	t
h	l	i	k	e	v	e
d	a	p	l	a	n	t

catch ☐ like ☐
create ☐ live ☐
dive ☐ plant ☐
eat ☐ travel ☐
help ☐ visit ☐

B Read each sentence and decide whether the verb is in the past or present tense. Tick the correct box.

	Past	Present
Turtles are in danger.	☐	☐
Dinosaurs lived millions of years ago.	☐	☐
Lots of animals like to eat turtles.	☐	☐
In 1980, about 115,000 female turtles laid eggs.	☐	☐

Non-fiction Vocabulary and spelling • Student Book page 119

Syllables and compound words

A Show how each word can be split up into syllables. The first one has been done for you.

jour/ney   jellyfish   travel

beaches   dangerous   fishing

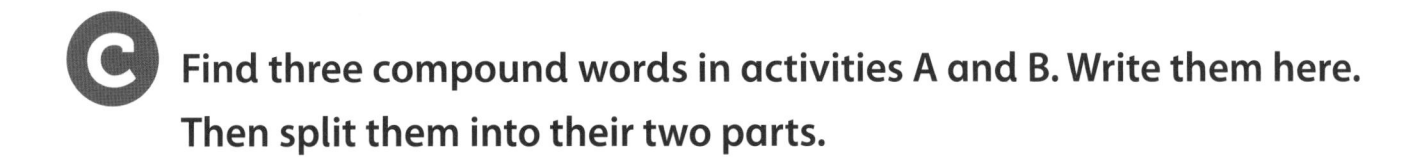

B Count the syllables in each word and write it in the correct box.

food   football   wild   endangered   turtle   leatherback

1 syllable	2 syllables	3 syllables

C Find three compound words in activities A and B. Write them here. Then split them into their two parts.

1 _____ = _____ + _____

2 _____ = _____ + _____

3 _____ = _____ + _____

75

Connectives

A Fit these connectives into the puzzle.

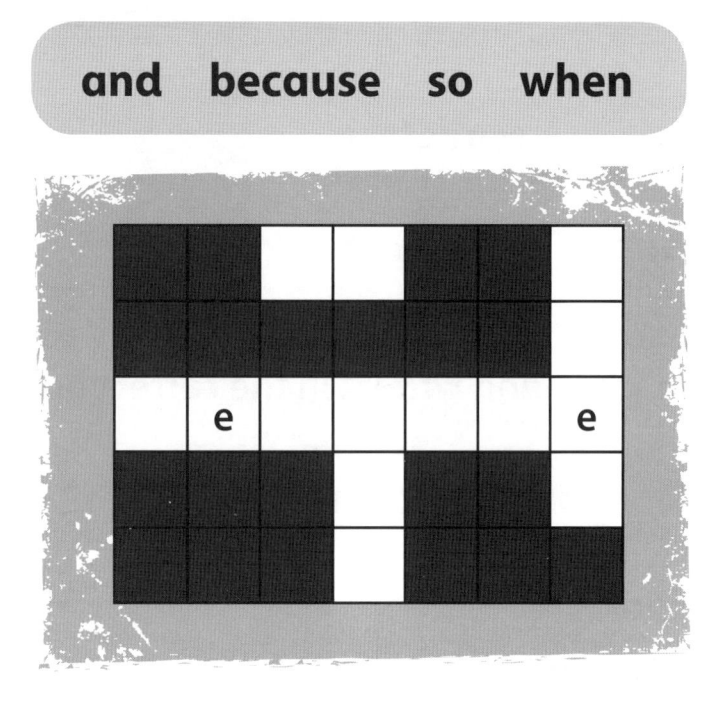

> and   because   so   when

B Choose the best connective from the puzzle to fill each gap.

1 Milo could not sit down _____ there were no empty chairs.

2 Granny was just going out _____ the phone started to ring.

C Write a sentence about a TV programme or a game you like. Use 'because' to explain what you like about it.

_____

_____

Non-fiction Grammar and vocabulary • Student Book page 127

Adjectives

A Look at these pictures of the endangered ivory-billed woodpecker. Underline the adjective in the caption for each picture.

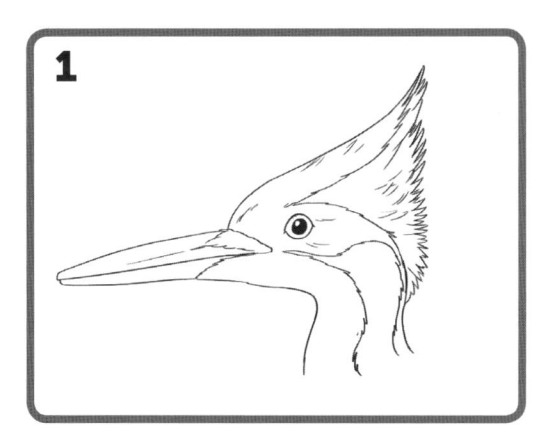

1. A pointed crest

2. A long bill

B Rewrite the captions in activity A using different adjectives. Choose words from below or think of your own.

> stunning   dazzling   enormous
> beautiful   magnificent   scarlet

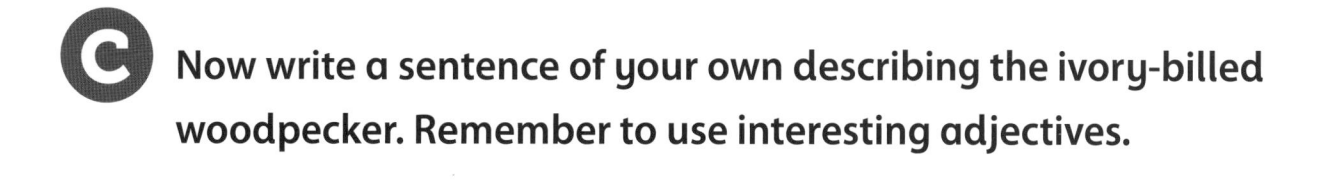

_____

_____

C Now write a sentence of your own describing the ivory-billed woodpecker. Remember to use interesting adjectives.

_____

_____

77

Non-fiction Writing • Student Book pages 128–129

Get writing

Use the information about leatherback turtles on pages 70 and 73 to fill in the chart.

Leatherback turtle facts

What is the problem? (Look at the paragraph 'Turtles in danger'.)	• • •
Where do they travel from and to? (Use the 'Longest journey' paragraph.)	•
How are they being helped? (Use the paragraph in activity C on page 73.)	• •

78

Non-fiction Assessment

Self-assessment on my learning
Unit 8 Animal world

Name _____ Date _____

☺ I understand and can do this well.

😐 I understand but am not confident.

☹ I don't understand and find this difficult.

Learning objective	☺	😐	☹
Reading skills			
I can find the features of reports.			
I can find answers to questions in different sections of text.			
I can find adjectives.			
Writing skills			
I am getting better at using past and present tenses.			
I can link ideas in sentences using connectives.			
Language (spelling) skills			
I can find the syllables in a word.			
I can split a compound word into parts.			

I would like more help with

_____

Poetry Reading • Student Book pages 130, 133, 134 and 137

9 Wordplay poems

Look at the children at the bottom of the picture. Start reading the poem from there.

Allivator

at the top.

then eat you

his back

ride upon

let you

he will

in a shop

see one

if you

allivator

Beware the

Roger McGough

80

A

1. Where might you see the allivator?

   _____

2. Where will the allivator let you ride?

   _____

3. What will happen at the top?

   _____

B 'Allivator' is a made-up word. Which two words are put together to make it? Tick the correct answer.

☐ alligator and stairs

☐ alligator and elevator

☐ elevator and anteater

C Why do you think the poet has set out the poem the way he has? Why does it start at the bottom?

_____

_____

_____

Poetry Vocabulary and spelling • Student Book pages 132, 136 and 139

Word detective

Look back at the poem 'Allivator' on page 80.

A What shape is the poem written in? Tick the correct answer.

a circle ☐   an elevator ☐   a tree ☐

B

1 Find the word in the poem that rhymes with 'top'.

_____

2 Write one or two other words that rhyme with 'top'.

_____

C

1 Find the word in the poem that has the long /igh/ sound.

_____

> Remember – the long /igh/ sound can be spelt in different ways:
> igh in high   i in find
> y in cry   i–e in ice
> ie in pie

2 Circle the words below that have the long /igh/ sound.

| kitten | hide | try | miss |
| kind | hill | light | eight |

Poetry Vocabulary • Student Book page 136

Descriptions

A Look back at the picture of the allivator on page 80. Now choose the six best words and phrases from the box below to describe it.

> spiky tail   big eyes   pointed claws   sharp teeth
> dark eyebrows   wet tongue   scary eyebrows
> large nose   tall   giant   long tail
> bulging eyes   dripping tongue

_____   _____

_____   _____

_____   _____

B Imagine the allivator is in a shop that you go to. Write a sentence describing the allivator. You can choose words and phrases from activity A or use words of your own.

_____

_____

C Now think of a word to describe the allivator's smile!

_____ smile

Poetry Phonics • Student Book pages 132 and 139

Sounds

A Draw lines to match the words that begin with the same sound.

slide	many
trick	why
sizzle	try
mine	sigh
whisper	slip

B Which five words in activity A have the long /igh/ sound?

_____ _____ _____

_____ _____

C

1 Use two of the words you matched in activity A in a sentence of your own.

_____

_____

2 Think of two other words that start with the same sound and use them in a sentence of your own.

_____

_____

Poetry Writing • Student Book pages 140–141

Get writing

Write a poem about an amazing new animal.

Part 1

Make up the name of a new animal by joining two words from the boxes below or use words of your own.

Tips:
You could join two words that rhyme.
You could join two words that begin with the same sound.

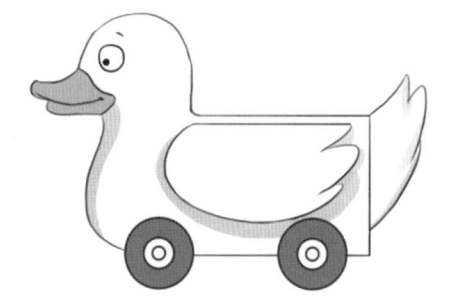

mouse
bear
crab
sheep
chicken

jeep
bridge
house
chair
taxi cab

New animal _____

Write some interesting words and phrases to describe the animal.

85

Poetry Writing • Student Book pages 140–141

Part 2

Plan your poem. Is it going to be a shape poem? Will your poem be wide or tall? Will it start at the top or at the bottom?

_____

_____

Decide if your poem is going to rhyme. Write down some words that rhyme with the words in your animal's name or in their description.

_____

_____

Part 3

Write your poem here using your best handwriting. Try to form your letters correctly and join the letters you have practised. You can use a separate piece of paper if you need more space.

_____

_____

_____

_____

Poetry Assessment

Self-assessment on my learning
Unit 9 Wordplay poems

Name _____   Date _____

☺ I understand and can do this well.

😐 I understand but am not confident.

☹ I don't understand and find this difficult.

Learning objective	☺	😐	☹
Reading skills			
I can find words that rhyme.			
I can find words that begin with the same sound.			
Writing skills			
I can use a poem I have read as a model for writing my own poem.			
Language (spelling) skills			
I can find words with the long /igh/ sound.			

I would like more help with

_____

_____

Learning reflections

What do you think?

Which story, poem or facts did you like best? Draw a picture below of something you enjoyed learning about.

Write two sentences about what you liked best and why.

_____

_____

_____

Word Cloud dictionary

Aa

abandon *verb* to leave something alone
angle *noun* a point of view
argue *verb* to quarrel
armour *noun* the metal coverings worn to protect people or things in battle
asparagus *noun* a green vegetable
atmosphere *noun* the feeling you get in a room or place

Bb

baklava *noun* a sweet dessert made from filo pasty
bamboo *noun* a tube-like plant that grows in China
blame *verb* to say someone has done something wrong
breadfruit *noun* a type of tree that has large round fruits
breeze *noun* a gentle wind
bulb-eye *adjective* describing an eye that bulges out

Cc

campsite *noun* a place where people stay in tents
candied *adjective* covered in sugar
CE *noun* the 'Common Era', meaning dates after the year-numbering system began
cinder *noun* a small piece of coal or wood that is partly burned
conceal *verb* to hide something carefully

concertina *noun* a portable musical instrument that you squeeze together and open up again to push air past reeds

conservationist *noun* a person who protects the planet, plants and animals

control room *noun* a room where the people in charge of something decide what to do

crater *noun* the mouth of a volcano

crouch *verbs* to bend down low with legs bent

Dd

decorate *verb* to make something look pretty and colourful

dozens *noun* a large number or amount (a 'dozen' is a group of twelve)

Ee

endangered *adjective* at risk of extinction

equal share *noun* the same amount

erupt *verb* to explode from the top

expression *noun* the look on a person's face

extinction *noun* when there are no more examples of an animal alive

Ff

flap *verb* to move from side to side or up and down

fluffiest *adjective* softest

Gg

gallop *verb* to run very fast

grasp *verb* to take hold of firmly

greenhouse *noun* a glass building that is kept warm inside for growing plants

Hh

henna *noun* a dye that is used to make patterns on hands in some countries

horror *noun* fearful shock

hostess *noun* a woman who has guests and looks after them

Jj

jaguar *noun* a large wild cat that is similar to a leopard and lives in South and Central America

jealous *adjective* wanting something that someone else has

jingle *verb* to make a tinkling sound

Word Cloud dictionary

Ll

landing *noun* the space between the rooms in the upstairs of a house

lava *noun* rock that is so hot it has turned into a red hot liquid

lengthwise *adverb* across the longest part of something

Mm

mansion *noun* a very large house

melt *verb* to make something a liquid

mozzarella *noun* an Italian white cheese that goes gooey when cooked

Nn

national park *noun* a large area of countryside which is protected by the government

nibble *verb* to take little bites

Pp

parting *noun* the line where hair separates into different directions

piñata *noun* a container filled with sweets or toys and hung up during parties and hit with a stick until it breaks open

plain *noun* an open area of grassland

pleat *noun* a fold that has been stitched into material

Rr

rake in the money *verb phrase* to earn lots of money
recite *verb* to say something out loud
recycle *verb* to reuse
reward *noun* something given to a person in return for something they have done
rim *noun* the edge
rock sample *noun* a piece of rock that has been collected and will be examined by scientists

Ss

sack *noun* a simple bag without handles
samosa *noun* a triangular savoury pastry containing vegetables or meat
sardine *noun* a small fish often sold in cans
scale *noun* one of the thin, overlapping parts on the outside of an animal
scene *noun* a setting
scruff of the neck *noun phrase* the back of the neck
scuttle-foot *adjective* describing feet that move fast
shabbiest *adjective* most scruffy or in poorest condition
shame *verb* to make someone feel ashamed
shape *verb* to give a particular shape or form to something
shiny *adjective* glossy and bright from reflected light
shoo *verb* to make someone or something go away by waving ones arms

silk *noun* a smooth, shiny cloth

singsong *adjective* having a repeated up and down rhythm, like the sound of singing

skim *verb* to move quickly over the top of something

skylark *noun* a bird that sings as it hovers in the air

slanted *adjective* sloping or leaning at an angle

slap *verb* to hit with the palm of the hand

slide *verb* to move slowly over a flat surface

smoky *adjective* filled with or covered in smoke

smoulder *verb* to burn very slowly

snatcher *noun* someone who takes things quickly

sorrow *noun* sadness

spread *verb* to make a thin layer of something

sprinkle *verb* to put tiny amounts over something

squawk *verb* to make a loud, harsh cry

startled *adjective* surprised

striker *noun* a football player who scores goals

swish *verb* to quickly sway from side to side

Tt

threaten *verb* to put in danger

tingle *noun* a feeling like little sparks

toxic *adjective* poisonous

tropical *adjective* found in the hot and humid regions near the equator

tug *verb* to pull hard

Vv

virtual world *noun* a world created on the computer

Ww

wash over *verb* to move over like water

wild boar *noun* a fierce type of pig that lives in the wild

winch drum *noun* a barrel that cable is wrapped around

wisdom *noun* sensible words

Word Cloud dictionary

New Word List

English word	Home language word or English definition